ALKALI SINK

ALKALI SINK

POEMS

STELLA BERATLIS

SIXTEEN RIVERS
PRESS

Published by Sixteen Rivers Press
P.O. Box 640663
San Francisco, CA 94164-0663
www.sixteenrivers.org

Library of Congress Control Number: 2014913803
ISBN: 978-1-939639-06-6

Design by Josef Beery

Cover art: U.S. Geological Survey Map,
Los Banos Quadrangle, California, 1916

Epigraph by Roberta Spear on page 1 from
A Sweetness Rising: New and Selected Poems, ed. Philip Levine
(Great Valley Books, 2007).
Reprinted by permission of Jeffery Shelby.

Contents

I

I know that it comes from the ground,
the jittery skin of hardpan.
But oh how the wind seems to own it,
making it rise and move through us
though we'd swear we'd seen nothing.

Roberta Spear
from "Dust"

Koda Farms, South Dos Palos

Rice loves the pixelated hills,
the valley oak in the center
of every orchard, silos
quivering in the distance,
cubic tons of highway grit
and thermal inversion
merging to a point
near Dos Palos, that whirl
of wanting, one valley south,
where inflorescence
dangles heavily in the paddies
like a pendulous goodbye.
I've missed you like breath,
like kernels of truth.
Let's meet in the fields
and grasp at heads of rice
turning ochre in the husks
while our central nervous systems
vibrate and hum like idling harvesters
waiting for the fields to drain.

Crop Rows in Autumn

This is how faces fall apart:
our eyes fixed to a point

somewhere on the flat horizon.
We walk in furrows of rich soil

for years, for a lifetime—
then start following the furrows

to the clouds. This is how lives
fall open: a man loves and hopes

while his wife shrinks
one acre per year; how love

weaves out: a cotton rope tensing
then raveling into many frayed strands,

its shining moments leftover gourds
strewn by the road after harvest.

But we forge ahead like physics,
until longing dissolves

the face, until systems
of measurement are obsolete

and we fix our eyes
on the vanishing point.

Fruit Barn with Goats and People

See the pretend family:
it enjoys gathering crisp leaves
while sitting under the weeping canopy
of late October. *This day is as cold*
as the ocean whorls, the mother says,
and this bowl of farm is mermaidful.
Now the father's anxiety is a llama rising to all fours
grazing on the weedy pastures of their life;
the child's voice a stripped willow branch
whistling through the wavy fall tableau,
a mixing stick for make-believe fires.
A lollipop makes it fun, says the child.

It's fall, and the goats are posing
in the endless valley.

Mustard Greens, Interstate 580

With enough olive oil and lemon juice,
it was easy for her to overlook the occasional
woody stem, their bitter tang:
roadside mustard, dandelion greens,
right there at the freeway's side—
first a bag, then the entire trunk stuffed
full. She came to carry a knife in the glove box
to cut the juicy weeds of this new country,
while her husband laughed
at the provincial poverty of it all—
eating greens that had been basking
in car fumes and animal piss—
yet for her, hunger was not just a distant thought
but a chemical memory in her muscles,
her jaws. And out here was a veritable *Sound of Music*,
the hills alive, nourishing the village she carried,
whispering *yes, we will feed you.* These are new
melodies of unyellowed mustard in early spring,
songs of fullness, love. The crunch underfoot as she scouts
the freshest bunch. The squeak of swaddling in clean
flour-sack towels. The drive back in the brown LeSabre,
shrugging off banana boat comments.
Later, at home, she washes up a sinkload
and boils it gently for an hour. Everyone eats.

Patterson Pass

This is the place that inhabits us,
the place where inversion, layering down,
spills water into trough and tap of valley—

Altamont of my rib, aqueduct of your chest,
            anchor of homes, totem of tract and sky
            tied up in blue's drawstring bag

below me   you   and sky above   all that dihedral flight
distilled down to seep-spring monkey flower.

This landscape has settled into a familiar refrain:
            kestrel   kite   shrike   redtail
            folding into the blade
            sometimes a crow

sometimes a man saying *hey*: an exhalation.

Here, uncertainty does not seem complex,
            loaded as it is onto crackling pallets
            and driven off to sub-stations of the West.

Wind, and how we don't understand the farming of it,
how the mills hum, moan, susurrate hoarsely,
how the skin cartwheels into windmills,
electromagnetic field.

Or the houndstooth scoring of riparian beds.

Or the sleek catwalk of girder.

We can't see the tomorrow-land of here,
only a cow's four feet
plugged into the hills.

Donut Shop at the End of the World

Inside the donut shop
at the end of the world,
she fills the dishwasher rack
with scratched flatware
and ponders her life of food service,
these waterlogged devotions;
wants to believe her attention
to the arrangement of utensils
matters in the world; people
demand spotless spoons
to stir their Coffee Mate
into bitter coffee.
That old man out front is holy—
see the focused way he washes
that section of sidewalk, the way
he scours the cement under the seats
clean as driftwood on the shores of this
secondhand island.
She and her hangnails
shouldn't be surprised;
this is a seminary for the streets:
wrinkled hands here in the water,
fingering utensils like rosaries,
the special of the day a miracle
seven days a week.

Memory's Nettles

Do you remember biting into
the soggy forkful
of dark stem-and-leaf,
tasting the startling sweetness

of Greek mountain afternoon? In that rocky lot
dotted with wild cyclamen, your sisters—
my aunts—walking slowly, pointing out
clumps with their knives. The oldest, my namesake

in widow's black, telling the story of boiled
nettles. The soldier who, missing his own
young daughter, wanted to adopt you.
We young women, always the American girls

with tied tongues and half-understanding smiles, know nothing
except the greens. That day we picked
armyra, italika, vlita, radikia; stuffed
our weeds into plastic bags and walked to Lia's,

where we removed the roots, bathed
the greens in a large zinc tub, and tossed
them into a pot of boiling water. I,
steak knife in my hand, racked my brain
for a word—remember?

When I See His Cane

He sleeps in the hallway, warding off
vengeful angels and thieving neighbors,
his voice rasping, *I fought in the war*
and I can't get any quiet in this house.
He sounds like the devil.

He eats his bowl of milk and bread,
arranges three blankets with care.
What matters now is milk and sleep.
He makes his bed on the couch.
In this house, he sleeps in the hall
but inhabits every room.

He recites the names of nineteen Cretan villages,
then presents me his cane.
A gift I don't want.
Enai pournari, he says, a tree
grown for its bent roots.

The cane's wood is lined, pitted, harder than chairs
broken over the backs of women and children.
Did he understand this fifty years ago,
as he led his daughters into hidden coves,
chased them onto wind-swept peninsulas,

shoulder-rode them into dark places?

Saddle-Soaping the Sofa

My sister commented on the terrible scratches
on the leather sofa, her toddler's game
of tic-tac-toe scratched into the light brown skin.
That's the truth, she said; *I can't control*
what that kid does. So from her box of shoe stuff
out came the saddle soap,
which, the label directs, must be worked
into a lather in the round tin
and applied with a clean white cloth,
next wiped with another, slightly damp.
While we polished, I told her, *he did it to me, too*,
and she just moved that cloth around and around
in a small circle. I never knew saddle soap could smell so clean,
so unbearably antiseptic—did you?
Why we didn't take opposite sides
for maximum efficiency, I don't know. Instead,
we worked right next to each other,
my cloth wiping next to her last swipe,
one cushion at a time, square by damp square. And she knew
I'd kept quiet in the stained days of accusation
and denial. We kept cleaning,
marveling at the dirt on the cloths,
how we both worked so hard
at our shared task.

How to Drink Metaxa at a Funeral: Instructions for Mothers and Daughters

Small stubs of paper in a wind tunnel. Hands reach out to grab at windstorm of tickets, slips of memory, a snippet—Stella tells her daughter, Demetra, the poem:

1. Find Footing

[Title Goes Here]

This is about my grandmother's funeral
in Athens: her name was Fyllio.
She died in January 2000 at eighty-two,
one year before you were born.
She was buried in the First Cemetery of Athens;
to get to it, you have to walk by the grave
of Melina Mercouri.

2. Root Yourself to the Earth

Triantafyllia: a Greek name derived from the Greek word *triantafyllos,* which means "rose." Originally a martyr from Magnesia in Greece, who chose to die rather than deny Christ. Nicknames and diminutives include Triantafyllis, Fyllis, Fyllios, Triantafyllenios, Linos.

At her funeral, my Thea Lia cried her head off,
moaned pitifully at the graveside,
hid it from no one,
was comfortable

with her terrible sadness.
Then the coffin lid was removed
for one last viewing.
They don't do cremation there;
the body is paramount—
they don't want you to touch the dirt at the gravesite.
The cats, you see . . .

3. Grasp the Shot Glass Firmly

When your grandmother Marika was eight, she buried a stillborn.
When she was twelve, she watched her grandfather take his last breath.
Then she helped her grandmother prepare his body for burial.

. . . and in that singular
overriding grief,
Lia passed out. *Aiera Aiera,*
the men ordered, their arms sweeping
invisible planes of air.

4. Briefly Imagine the Loved One in Her Final State

Interior Viewing Room, Late Afternoon

Iosif limps his way through the small room toward the raised casket. Photos, candles, an announcement: everything has been examined here, except for the woman in the casket. Iosif stoops to pick up a slip of paper from the floor while Stella speaks to her mother.

Stella (whispering)
I don't remember what I'm supposed to say now.

Maria
Zio se mas.
Life to us.

5. Knock It Back in One Shot

So I stood there, Demetra, looking at Fyllio,
your great-grandmother,
whose name grows from *rose*
and links to "love of all mankind"
and "love of horses"
and "the science of kissing,"
and I remembered how she'd pet my arm,
how her own arms shook as she rolled out dough
for the Easter pastry, *kalitsounia.*
I remembered how I discovered that
her gaze behind those closed lids
was its own branch of science,
the most ancient part of the universe
in the wood of her rolling pin

Orange Grove RV Park

The monarchs are migrating this spring.
Larry has washed them off the windshield several times
at rest stops between Modesto and Bakersfield,
and now he carefully scrapes the brazen expanse
again—the third time—at this RV park,
where the shtick is all-you-can-pick
oranges. The smell overwhelms as we pull in—
the narcotic scent of citrus honey only adults seem able
to detect. My mother inhales and moans, rapturous,
as my daughter shrieks, *I can't smell it, I can't smell it,*
her dismay squeezing the air out of my chest like
a very tight hug. Some time later, Larry still ministering
to the glass, we collect citrus blooms, follow a lizard
along a stack of railroad ties, and analyze how we might play
on an oversized concrete pipe randomly placed in sand.
The heat and exhaustion scour me clean. Above,
a helicopter buzzes in ever-widening circles in
weak yellow skies, a manhunt in neighboring groves.
The windshield is now filmed with new dust.
I sit on a picnic table, its flakes of blue peeling paint
catching the weft of my pants, while the generations
who sandwich my life skip and slide, *korai*
in the sun-baked gravel, maidens in the trailer park.

When We Completely Lose Our Bearings

My life is opening like an umbrella, Diane,
but it's an umbrella with a ferrule tip, rips, and a splintered crook
handle. The fabric: patterned with navy ribbons of regret,

secret scarlet surgeries with crunchy snow before, after, and under,
thrown Depression glass and plaster wall dents (lovingly rendered!),
and packages of reducing candy. All printed on the bonnet; true story.

And the tube—carved all around with sorry acts, lies I may have told,
times I took one for the team. Let's not forget the stretchers,
leveling out to support each rib as the runner slides up the tube,

the yawning architecture beneath a sanctuary for hummingbirds, lost children,
and the unmotivated, just hanging around. The structure's like a rainforest
with separate layers of existence: in the canopy, household lemurs wash dishes,

the lesser capybara rummages the bottom shelves looking for the large bottle
of Seagram's. At this point in time, we may have forgotten our opposable digits.
Fuckin' evolution, Diane (if that is your real name); my fingers get pinched in a clutch.

Pray what? Give me succor, O umbrella, protect me from *bukake*
and handguns of lust; torrents of rain; save me from the world's gusts
that turn me inside out: mistral, diablo, katabatic—
holy crap, a world tour of the winds? I'm in!

Desert Lichens of Gabbs, Nevada

A particular scanty specimen
coats empty beer cans and dead vegetation,
landscapes or persons hither and thither,
those damaged or scarred or wrapped in chains,
just holding together: packets of energy, tidy quanta.
All the tethers harden over geologic time—explain that!—and fossilize
into the soft tissue of the corporal body.
Time, that space-time, brittles us all
while we soar with it to the frontiers of seeing and knowing,
and those who travel closer to the ends of things we cannot yet name,
who have flown through it all, more cell-dead.
And for what? Meteorites? Feldspar? That one green we saw
on every hillside? The cool breath of the Earth's center
and this larger darkness to be loved? I'll insist,
in this valley of arson, on the sun's blinding glare,
and ten or twelve hours per day acting like lichen
on wind-dried rocks—O the days—yes! Imbibe, then capillary,
then action: we belong exactly there, sucking water from the air.

Cultural Anthropology

Where acres divide and subdivide—
that's where I lived. With dusty front yards,
trenchers at the ready to dig channels
and lay miles of pipe. On the next block
nothing but fields of yellow straw and foxtail whips,
dirt tracks and spindly pine, eucalyptus,
and garbage piles heaved over suburban
fences. Along the outlines of human
habitat is where we sifted for goods—
in majestic cones of garbage
you could find sharp broken tiles,
rusty nails harboring tetanus,
deadly fist-sized mortar chunks,
spiky rebar threads,
and the occasional beer pull tab,
crusted saliva from who knows where
ready for DNA testing. A chip of dirt-marbled
dinner plate, poised to hurl and slice, next to the
stiff pelt of the neighbor's missing cat.
A pleasant town, a town of progress,
where acres divide and divide again.

I heard on the radio

they are blowing up the sugar plant, so
we drive north to a town of old sharp smells.
The nose tells us we've reached Manteca,
olfactory curiosity, but also the clean rows of
a Greek farmer's vines. In this town, owl decoys

perch on buildings, vigilant with glass eyes.
Airstream trailers peek out behind eucalyptus teeth
and bid hello to the truck drivers who are always
just passing through. We plow

through it all, ferment-stink as
sugar beets roast on slow-moving belts—
and behind that odor, the oil burn of gears that turn efficiently
twenty-four hours a day. But today, all this has given way

to a man saving his place at the chain-link carnival
that surrounds this temple,
and a barker who announces the winner
of a contest to push the plunger
that detonates the charge
that begins the demolition
we've come to witness.

The ceremony starts: a collective twitch
as staccato charges snap the air—
loosening creaky spines and unlacing steel ribbons.

But those old towers hang in the air, stubborn,
releasing dust and exhaling possibility—

then the fall and spill upon the earth.

When the dust clears, we wander back,
desolate, looking for a place,
like people wondering
where to get their next meal,
like the silver pigeons
who have lost a good home.

17th and F Subterranean, with Horn Section

There's a happiness in this room,
as we listen to the drivers of
Loomis armored cars
rev engines and honk horns

in the parking lot next to your
underground home.
There's heaven in the armored cars

and in knowing that safety exists
here, adjacent to diamonds and green millions,
next to the parking lot where engines race
and drivers lean on the horns: get out of the way.

The basil plant in the window
absorbs sound waves,
thrives on the thud

of industry and commerce and engines,
while value is being shifted
from one part of town to the next
and people amble from one spot to the next

and we sit here, you and I, receiving the sound waves
that feed the plant and vibrate the walls of this home,
which exists just under the street

Crestline Road

I remember it as fever's living quarters,
the place where I suffered, daubing my forehead
with wet cloths, becoming as intimate
with the slender tube of mercury as I'd become
with the arguments from my parents' room.

One night after their divorce, I panicked, tried to run
out into open January with a 106-degree fever.
They pulled me back inside, my mother
and Patty Plato, the lady from work—and teamed up
to catch me at either end of the loopy floor plan.

I dodged them by floating to the starry ceiling
that rainbowed this broken family world,
the acoustic popcorn harboring me,
a mere wisp of dust in the hazardous household air.
My point of view shifted to the highest altitude,

and I saw my body running, a dot
rounding the track of our home's vicious cycle.
My body stubbed its toe on a chair,
and the pain sucked me back,
a panting genie sitting on the kitchen counter,

heat dissipating from all that wasted orbiting.
I rested there before being led to the cold bath.
Not yet glue, or ice, but exhibiting
all the properties of an incoming fireball
quietly gathering force inside my skin, inside those walls.

II

The world is bound with secret knots.

Athanasius Kircher
Magneticum naturae regnum

Quince Theory

Just do a straight hardwood cutting.
Place them into a large glass vase.
These are sticks, sticking straight up.

There's a conflicted pleasure
in how the sap can flow in the branch,
disembodied from the shrubby heart.
Wait for the buds to open. So alive,
a sea monkey that wakens in water,
O monstrous. O propagation.

I'll never tire of these stems
orphaned from the root-ball,
severed from the mycorrhizal web

as if nothing else mattered.
For those of us missing symbiosis
with its fungus and host plants,

we're sad figures who stick to it,
queen bees, parthenogenitors
of our own aquariums, brine-shrimp land—

or trapped inside snow globes,
our handsome cuttings loud, self-mothering,
as we push into tiny new spaces.

On the Subject of the Crawl Space

As the name suggests, kiddo, a crawl space
is a sort of basement. Should the room

be a mushroom? The floor, a drama
of spores? Wherefore? You say

the room's height was as low
as your childhood—hey! I worked hard

to carve out that space. The resident mole's
bum ankle kept you up at night, you say?

Could've been worse: Look at me
in my early days. Now, disperse, go away.

I'm your mother, and I'm not thinking
about stalks, caps, and volvas. My pickax trembles.

All the Clothes She Has Ever Sewn

Look back at this chunky lace scene:
this holy toile that shades off, flaxen,
at the edges—
a mottled view through pinhole
aperture.
E-lab-o-rate.
Make elaborate;
trim and adorn skeletons and
fade them into translucence;
onion skin, papers to be worn.
Erase the bony edges
and celebrate the marrow,
the sorrow, Theotokos—
with convictions in organdy
and satin and a belief in metallic sin.
O she who gives birth to pleats,
to ribboned seams and silky sundries, to panels
and heart-sore tears in the lace, whose thread
bunches and who starts again
from the zigzag edge,
from every beginning to almost-finished
loves: only she is worthy
of these little squares
scissored with gusto;
only she makes the cut.

Dinner, Interrupted by Paperboy

In the Middle East and even less fertile areas, there are sheep and goats.
So it was in California, the skulls of two lambs on a plate
one night with company. You'd be surprised
what a roasted head looks like: the eyes an unlikely white,

long tongues in permanent loll, cheeks roasted to juicy
rounds. All of us sat around the table: my wife, my ma,
Kokkinos and his woman, and Buranis with the blind eye
staring at nothing. When the doorbell rang, my wife jumped,

upsetting the table: glasses of wine teetered,
the flatware chinked against itself—and for a moment, *koritsi mou*,
we stared as those lamb heads wobbled in the center of the table.
When everything settled, she rushed for a clean white towel,

whirled and draped it over the table, magician style, concealing
our pagan feast. Later, Kokkinos, carving out the tongue, said,
"So much of what's delicious requires work on the part of the eaters."
Yes. Here's to Kokkinos, dying of the cancer now, inside every one of his bones:

a split skull is a gift. This offal, the world's heart and soul,
transformed by sleight of hand and time.

The Chevy Truck of Yore

Every time I drive past it,
the '49 Chevy half-ton,
the one I sold last year.

The one I sold last year,
brown fenders, cream body,
rebuilt 327 engine.

He rebuilt that 327 engine
over the course of years
spent sitting in the driveway.

Sitting with beer in the driveway,
tank top and tools spread out around—
the thing will run someday.

That son of a bitch did run for the first few years;
I impressed some boys,
then parked it for good.

Parked it for a decade,
fluids separating into parts;
part me, part you, part glue.

The Rambler Ambassador of Yore

Glistening eyes at 4 A.M.,
parked-car standoff,
diesel trucks lumbering past,
purposeful and loaded.

Push-button transmission lights glow on the dash,
and she stares at those tiny lights. They are
the sunrise, the savior, daybreak, the flood
receding as trucks sigh fumes and lullabies.

The lights. She will push the buttons and
they will yield under a finger, the clutch
will slip, the gear engage, she will slip under,
hygienic paper sheath crinkling
under the weight of buttocks resting
there. Let your knees fall open.

Later, it's the glistening eye, the standoff;
the parked car, the accusation, her triumphant escape—
driving off, purposeful and loaded, carrying
a new secret for the future:
a hard kernel of something, a smooth oval pebble,
a single burning cell, a light in mineral eyes.
A memory,
this implanted thing,
vibrating beneath its protective cover.

A Little Tête-à-Tête with Desire, Eternity, and a Cabbage

The future's
an uncertain kohlrabi:
barefaced geometry born
of heat waves,
impossible
crisscross
and divergent line
from yesterday's
breadth—
a *now* situated
between two points:
those boundaries, fixed,
but expansive as a cabbage,
as an unconstrained love
unfolding, guided by voices,
but something infinite, like a blank page,
a page to which something unruly
is sent, with repercussions,
that thin crown of leaves,
sweet and bare
and noisy.

A Certain Tree Confined to North America

Velvety underside and five-toothed leaflet,
single-seed samara winging down, ash—
Fraxinus velutina—
shading thinly,

and once, before language's bumpy tongue,
something like the wind touched my cheek
and you canopied my face and whispered
    curtain-leaf
    stillroot
    branchlet

your deciduous tendencies revealed
like green light on sidewalk
(which can be luminous, too),
the names of things and their pulpy centers.

The Gardener Ponders Death and Basil

Beneath a lodgepole arbor
you pot basil seedlings
in your patched down coat and watchman's cap,
carefully placing shards of clay
to block the soil from washing out the drain.

One summer you kept a special eye on
someone else's Mediterranean garden:
Russian sage, lavender, olive trees, red salvia,
a husband dying in a rented bed in the living room,
a wife who refused to water one living thing.

You even touched his body once or twice,
helped to clean him, turn him over onto his side;
it was like watering a summer's worth of herbs,
potting up a lifetime of Japanese maple saplings,
or pinching off the flowers of two hundred basil plants.

You'll soon hand over the little black pots
to anyone who fancies them, anyone who wants
to grow an herb or two.
Sitting on your tree-stump stool,
you watch the unlikely steam
rising from the compost.

Passing into One and Out of Another

I wish for the incinerated
table-top muffin tin

that you called art,
a cocky crow

playing its beady eye
at your jam sessions.

I wish for another
January 24,

one more crop
of Sweet 100s,

ice cream
in the pedestrian Valley heat,

stuffed crows,
burnt foods,
miniature rocking chair,

a wishing well
at your front door.

All this extra time.

How to Identify Skulking and Ambiguous Birds

I am learning the art of *pishing,*
          she said.

I can scold like a titmouse,
          whinny like a screech-owl,

and emit pure shrill
          as I see fit.

Meet me in the tree house
          in the trembling leaves
                    and I'll . . .

What sort of weather are you, I asked?

          I am like most weathers, waiting

          to crack walnuts with crows
                    and swoop like the Cooper's hawk—

waiting, she said,
          for tongues, vowels,
and spit
to summon me.

Vitreous Detachment

One hundred years ago, cows munched
on this dark slope.
How do I know?
Mule's ears.
Disturbed soils.
And up in the air?
Pinpoints of infrared,
memory of light
organized by gazers,
chaos explainers.
One year ago I left you
and I saw flashes
with my eyes closed.
My humor will grow slack
like my skin, my throat;
I can measure
mass for proof—
stoichiometry.
Strands vibrate inside my eyes
where the other disengagement
takes place. Float me.
On the hill where we mutely
grazed, the chokecherry star—
nothing's more beautiful than
flashes we see with eyes closed.

Hawk Moth

O, to live
like some larvae:
to fold up neatly
into one self
to wrap up
then exfoliate
the past
forgive
what is to come
give birth
to one's own
metamorphosis:
a five-spot wing,
immaculate.

What I Understood

I understood you three months ago,
even three days ago,
but now you're a locomotive
speeding through a native West,
changing the scale of my earth—
what I think I want—
I can't grasp the principle of you.

If electrons and protons cannot
fix firmly to their atomic stations,
so too the wandering paths
of desire and fury.
Where did they go?
What road will they travel?

Three days ago I understood you
before your limbs unfurled
in random fashion,
before your syntax dissolved
into a barefoot shuffling sideways
across the dirt.

Finally, a Map of All the Body's Microbes

Turns out we're 10 percent human
and 90 percent bacteria.
Science has a map; each nook
is populated by smidgens of desire.
This often works to the advantage
of desire. Mornings,
the buggy specks want coffee, take it
black. But do not despair the lack
of decorum between you and the microbes.
We are colonies, manifold souls—
multiple selves swarm at the borders.

Prayer for Ye of Little Faith

Baby, my mouth's ripening
like a two-day-old plum on the counter,

and my antique hat is askew on my
foam head, crooked from wanting,

and we stand, hand in hand, overlooking the spot
where we'll soon be buried, so I

swoon and fall, alive with dying,
sweet and oozing, wrinkled skin folds—

incredulity the closest
we come to a prayer.

III

Getting lost was not a matter of geography so much as identity, a passionate desire, even an urgent need, to become no one and anyone, to shake off the shackles that remind you who you are, who others think you are.

Rebecca Solnit
A Field Guide to Getting Lost

Raisin Queen

I want to be
the Raisin Queen of Fresno,
and I'm taking concrete steps to get there.

Curled hair and rouged cheeks,
fine enunciation,
and a good dress are required.

A Raisin Queen is given latitude:
I can take a leave of absence
from my duties,

hike the Appalachian Trail—
I can go to Flagstaff—
then maybe cross national borders.

But on this first day
I'll stand at the town square flagpole in my festival attire,
a goddess of the raisin trade.

The photo shows a girl
lost inside her dreaming,
imagining salami and beer
and one of her dead fathers.

Nature vs. Nurture

In those days, we had no idea
our father was a drug dealer, not really.
Inside his house in a small briefcase
by the kitchen table

were little white packets of cocaine,
baggies of pot. One day, in our early teens,
my sister and I sat alone on the front porch
while our father was at work

butchering meat at the local Safeway.
His neighbor, who stood on a small ladder
trimming his crape myrtle,
exposed himself to us.

When we saw his penis swinging loose
in the space of his open fly,
we ran inside the house
where we debated briefly

before calling the police.
As we waited for the cops to show,
we sat at the Formica table
trying to make sense

of the whole situation,
wondering if we'd made
the right decision, if a man could
knowingly trim shrubs with his penis

dangling there, in the open,
if a father could really keep
a loaded gun behind the front door.
How easily danger becomes

part of the household,
a silly joke about poking
some whores, a favorite uncle—
no one thinks to shield your eyes.

Return to the Scene

At night he returns,
falls off the wagon,
and commences his bender.
He's 'round back
at the El Rancho,
sitting on the bumper
of an Econoline van.
He rushes around
his inside track,
the spinning motion
nudging him over and out,
away from the milk cans
and slapping hands,
the aprons hanging,
the home-brewed harpies.
He adds more liquid.
The night carries him off,
distilled
into
another
substance
altogether.

Elegy for a Mole

How naïve—I was scared to touch it.
This mole, stuck in the pipe
sunk down in our sandy soil
when it should be
tunneling miles under sod, tomato,
and bustling bolting-lettuce cities,
conducting digging business. In one myth,
a mole, eager to assist God
in universe-weaving, lets out too much thread
until finally Earth grows too large for the space
under heaven. It's like the space held
under this roof, unknowable in its vastness.
There are people here we are meeting
for the first time. Did we mismeasure our lives?
What to do? I do know this:
everything we do is wrong. Feed it a carrot.
Add batting to the hole.
Now its ghost whispers advice
from the pipe: *here's how you patch*
your world.

One Afternoon While Shredding Bank Statements

Unfold statements, line up checks
wide fingerprint lines
thick meat-cutting hands
butcher knife, casually palmed.

Fishing the canals
sleeping in chairs in the middle of the day
evenings in the interrogation room
confessing murder in your dreams.

Unfold statements, line up checks
Women's Center
Louie the Plumber
Jail on Wednesday
mother's house on Saturday.

Open the cell doors
throw away the knives
stop digging holes in the garden
and dragging the canals
the body has been located.

It's here, on the floor
in one or two thousand pieces
little shreds of evidence
of your work-furlough life.

Hank Senior

If you were alive,
you'd be walking in an alley at 4 A.M.,
slinking off to dark corners
with the queen of the rodeo.
With your guitar slung over your shoulder
and a voice that cuts like prairie wind,
coarse and honest, like an apron
hanging on a peg.

But you do walk here,
ambling along drive-thru church
parking lots and truck-stop diners,
wherever tongue and brain are sold from rusty steel trucks
and fat is fried crisp.
You're at the flea market, El Rematito,
where sunburned men from Texas
tell their life stories in halting verse.
In dark smoky bars where women mosey over
and whisper sour-breathed promises.
Outside, where men stoop over crops,
wrecked hands wiping brows.
When lovers fight and throw clothes in the lane
at Westward Ho Mobile Homes,
when the phone rings in the middle of the night
and a woman's voice says *Keep away from my man,*
when the needle scrapes the label at the album's quiet end,
you are there.

Little Cancers

And there you stood with your little cancers
popping up over skinny shins
like road blooms spinning dizzily,
electrifying the air with hisses and sly whistles
while the Mexican bird of paradise
bobbed its red-flowered stems,
a loud handkerchief waving us off.

Next to these fancy fireworks, what can compare—
an angry letter in the nightstand, a bad father now dead,
worry beads in your pocket, a mountain of chestnuts to climb?
Things need to be done, documents revised and signed,
biopsies performed, cells notarized—

but you cannot seem to bring yourself
to stop snipping slender agave spines
or separating chicks from hens
or beating the dirt with a little hand axe
to kill this thin orange day.

Ode to a Blood Relation

O, Departed Mind, how I've missed
you. I'm thinking about your bird calls
in ritzy restaurants, your curio nest
of figurines, and your careful attention

to shoe shopping. You navigated the body through
some tricky spots, like the bunion of '85
and persistent jet lag. You drove your hair
to be styled once a week and wondered

if the stylist were gay. Sometime, mind,
I'd like to take you to dinner,
feed you food high in antioxidants,
stimulate your lymphatic system and

watch you come 'round to linear thought. But
sequential's hard to find these days, like finding
a good cleaning lady. And linear might
steal the jewelry and move to Palm Desert.

Therefore, under the circumstances,
single-topic out-of-order thought
will suffice, such as "help change me the sheets"
or "gamble, leave casino."

If you were feeling cooperative, mind,
I might clothe you in organic cotton
and guide you through gentle stretching so
muscle memory, that good Samaritan, might pick up

your slack. Listen, mind—come back, all is forgiven!
I miss your wisdom on the topic of upholstery,
and no one's sent me a Hallmark card for years.
I've bought the Chardonnay

and promise I won't care about the level of the bottle
at three o'clock. I've vacuumed your carpets
with the nap to the left, here in your house,
where Hummel lambs lie waiting.

On the Way to the Funeral

We should not talk about death any more.
We should not.

Instead tell me about razor strops, Freemason pins, spectacles, key
fobs, a full-body cast for broken bones and words. Tell me about
your entire family standing on the back porch. Screen door.
Wood for building. Wood for burning.

Explain to me drawers full of cuff links, castings, findings, leavings,
monocles, a neon denture sign, any piece of redwood fresh
or worm-rotted gray.

Discuss your silver—beautiful silver, bent or fragmented, each
piece winking and damaged in some secret way: broken brooch,
lost earring, olive fork with crooked tine, tarnished goblet.

Tell me about the salvation of sterling in a junkyard bin.

Woman at Window

It didn't seem dangerous
sitting naked in front of the window
whose cracks had not yet begun to show,
the glass a liquid membrane
any arm could penetrate,
but she knew how to play it cool,
would not become a full-throated
embracer of theories, models, idioms,
and paradigms, would remain idiosyncratic
and try to take down the system
while working within it.
Vines would not entwine her.
Going undercover was risky work:
learning the lingo from the masters,
reviewing tapes to get it just right,
putting all her studious nature into play,
changing her voice to fit the role of
sitting naked in front of the window.
It was tough work to avoid family and
neighbors, and still perform the domestic duties
such as loving a child, and a husband, and
preparing meals, preparing them for strangers
and not-strangers. After all the training,
her body became magnetic, attracting danger
like iron filings and charged ions,
compelling all eyes.

Evidence of the Heart's Existence

Until such time as she is thoroughly
analyzed and dismantled, she might walk into

the world's longest-running general store
with straw in her fucked-up hair,

having forgotten her wallet
and boundaries out in the shed

in the backyard of that different
city, the one where trust abides. All footprints

lead to Forklift, California, the place of
thrift barns, dollar-store shoelaces, and eye hooks.

That place where even the chalk outlines
are dissociated, where books are stacked a foot high

on nightstands, where bloodstains and DNA
illustrate the workings of the nervous system on that day.

She continues to buy honey at the feed store
and shop at the local newsstand, out but hidden;

recons the quietest shade by the river's edge,
where the grass is high and uncrushable,

right near the houses, right under your nose,
to the place where thoughts cease and hearts start their blind beating.

Fire Safety Fact Sheet

Sometimes, there's a fire and it burns everything.
Other times, only the incidentals:
the lawnmower, the tandem bike: ash.
Then darker conflagrations, those embedded
inside the memory of the house: fire occludes,
a match is held against a child's skin,

a lesson for wetting the bed. It's always been
a time of burnings, of going flash-blind.
Now a child in the car watches the spreading blaze
from the passenger window. Tell her that you will return,
tell her not to exit, that everything will be fine when she cries
I always knew this would happen.

Still Life with Thud and Falter

It hits the windshield, thud
of bone and maybe fur,
and first you think, deer?
but then explosion of feathers, the way
they gather, slow motion, into
an arrangement you begin to cipher,
how they seem to settle
in mid-sky, motes in a sun patch.
Now the rushing air pulls them
to the edge, and you're back to the bird,
a pheasant, faltering wing and neck
before you, the feathers floating
impossibly, a frame.

Not About Engines or Physics

A 1927 Model T rushes forward,
the physics of its speed
able to move small bodies
with a brief, passionate roar.
First, windshield, then ascension, then the road.
Ligament, bone, and paper plates of tacos
break up slo-mo in the valley air: carnitas.
In the gutters, beer cans of the fathers,
in the street, a girl on a Honda.
She doesn't want to ride it,
but she will. Remember, children:
all instruction is brief and slurred,
you must remember to execute
seven things at once: brake, clutch, shift,
head check, signal, turn, roll on—
and beware of vehicles
with exposed engines:
they remind us how flimsily
a structure hangs together.

You Say Brit Bikes Are the Worst

Your Alfa Romeo, your Ducati,
your Vespa—*bella!* Your speed limit

is no limit, wide open throttle;
maximum power output,

going up the damn hills! Which means:
ready to seize at will. Freeze up, stop,

heart still, vanished for days
on the sides of roads,

where there's plenty of time
to ponder Bernoulli's equation,

inside of which is hidden
the past, which you've informed me

can never be erased.
It bears repeating:

the engine, O the engine,
is a rusted-metal something on a tarp;

an inclined barrel,
a gear tower that towers over us all:

you're subject to jet whims,
carburetor manuals on shelves,

and items in various states
of dismantle; you are subject

to grease and tobacco-stained hands,
rituals of beer and smoke,

tethered to no past.
The downshift, the motion,

time bent—you are
on entropy's agenda.

Turning Off the Flashlight in Golden Pen Mine

After driving through dry lightning
and hillside fire-strikes,
I'm crouching in the dirt,

listening to a voice, the words as fast as the flashlight beams
on the mine walls. *Whatever you knew before about dark,*

erase those tapes. Because now
your ass has been kicked by Real Dark.
So sit down, I'm turning off the lights.

And out the flashlight goes. I keep my eyes open
for the horror, the terror, so that I may understand

the body is nothing, negative infinity, sitting
under this mountain now and always.
The cells in my head fire off useless memos

as pretty little clods tumble down
onto my shoulders. Later, emerging into the day,

I grieve for the accident
I was sure would happen
when I followed the voice in.

Out of Hawthorne, Nevada

We benchmark-mapped it last week,
this mutilated mountain crest,

this dark night of the soul
for the sole traveler—but the maps lacked savvy,

could not predict the present dust storm. I might
hunker down inside the car off the unmarked

highway, on the invisible gravel
next to the other gravel,

and die. But I descend into these wilds, this out-of-range
place on the flats, race the Big Storm with its white flashes

and goldmine Goth panorama. Soon,
I'll pass the sign for Rawhide Road,

proof I am lost, forever lost in the desert of adrenaline
and alkali sink, no beer-bottle vase of lavender

to point the way at the mythical crossroads like you said
there would be, no search and rescue,

no gun in the waistband of your trousers.
I am watched from a distant rise,

the sky all virga and smudge, the dry thunderstorms
in both my homes, waiting.

Prayer to Ward Off Radiation and the Heart's Inconstancies

God! I have stood here waiting for clouds
to render in fast motion, while little snakes rear
at my doorstop and writhe, aurorae borealis
arcing from domestic erratics of the last ice age.

I have not told anyone anything or taken any oaths
that You did not previously authorize. But when gravity
forces me down and the charged particles
bombard the Earth and my body on it, that's when

I feel every star and rock inside me.
Surely, as knower of the unseen,
You are aware of the slurry. Help me
remember why I love what's under the leaf,

in dark corners, hiding horrors I can love. Forgive me—
for I know that every molecule comes from without,
created from the so-called nothing and fused into the one knot
just under my breastbone: the question of coronal ejection,

the cause of that sudden brightening, visible to the naked eye,
which illuminates the several darknesses of the heart.

Acknowledgments

I am grateful to the following publications in which these poems appeared, sometimes in slightly different versions: *California Quarterly:* "Out of Hawthorne, Nevada"; *Collision 2009:* "Mustard Greens, Interstate 580," "Still Life with Thud and Falter," and "On the Way to the Funeral"; *Collision 2010:* "Crop Rows in Autumn" and "Donut Shop at the End of the World"; *The Dirty Napkin:* "Quince Theory"; *hardpan:* "I heard on the radio"; *More Than Soil, More Than Sky: The Modesto Poets* (Quercus Review Press): "Koda Farms, South Dos Palos," "Orange Grove RV Park," and "Mustard Greens, Interstate 580"; *Penumbra:* "Memory's Nettles"; *The Place That Inhabits Us: Poems of the San Francisco Bay Watershed* (Sixteen Rivers Press): "Patterson Pass"; *Quercus Review:* "Crestline Road"; *Snail Mail Review:* "Saddle-Soaping the Sofa; *Song of the San Joaquin:* "The Gardener Ponders Death and Basil" and "Raisin Queen"; *Squaw Valley Review:* "Vitreous Detachment"; *Stanislaus Connections:* "Cultural Anthropology" and "Hawk Moth."

"Crop Rows in Autumn" and "Donut Shop at the End of the World" were reprinted in *More Than Soil, More Than Sky: The Modesto Poets* (Quercus Review Press). "Raisin Queen" was reprinted in *Stanislaus Connections* for "A Gathering of Voices."

Thanks to my family for their love and support, especially my mother, Marika; my sister, Dena; and my daughter, Demi. For her guidance and encouragement in writing this book, I am immensely grateful to Gillian Wegener. Thanks to Dana Koster for her poem "Kablooey," which inspired "When We Completely Lose Our Bearings."

Notes

An alkali sink, also known as a salt flat or a *salina*, is a habitat found in the desert and in some parts of the California Central Valley. The alkali sink habitat is hot and dry, and plant species that thrive there have adapted to grow in the salt-crusted hardpan.

In "Memory's Nettles," *armyra*, *italika*, *vlita*, and *radikia* all refer to types of *horta*, or wild spring greens, foraged in most parts of Greece.

In "How to Drink Metaxa at a Funeral: Instructions for Mothers and Daughters," the word *kalitsounia* refers to the small, sweet cheese pie which is a specialty of cooks on the island of Crete.

In "Orange Grove RV Park," *korai* is the plural of the Greek *kore*, an ancient Greek statute of a clothed young woman standing with feet together. *Koritsi mou*, in "Dinner, Interrupted by Paperboy," means "my girl."

Sixteen Rivers Press is a shared-work, nonprofit poetry collective dedicated to providing an alternative publishing avenue for San Francisco Bay Area poets. Founded in 1999 by seven writers, the press is named for the sixteen rivers that flow into San Francisco Bay.

SAN JOAQUIN • FRESNO • CHOWCHILLA • MERCED • TUOLUMNE
STANISLAUS • CALAVERAS • BEAR • MOKELUMNE • COSUMNES
AMERICAN • YUBA • FEATHER • SACRAMENTO • NAPA • PETALUMA